THE little girl WHO GAVE ZERO FUCKS

With special thanks
to Mymedia

THE little girl WHO GAVE ZERO FUCKS

WRITTEN BY AMY CHARLOTTE KEAN
ILLUSTRATED BY J. MILTON

U

unbound

First published in 2018
This paperback edition first published in 2020

Unbound
6th Floor Mutual House, 70 Conduit Street, London W1S 2GF

www.unbound.com

Text Design by Carrdesignstudio.com

A CIP record for this book is available from the British Library

ISBN 978-1-78352-946-9 (trade pbk)
ISBN 978-1-78352-645-1 (trade hbk)
ISBN 978-1-78352-644-4 (ebook)
ISBN 978-1-78352-646-8 (limited edition)

Printed in Slovenia by DZS Grafik

1 3 5 7 9 8 6 4 2

To Bethan, Sophie and Cecily.

I wrote this book for you (which according to Father Christmas is worth at least three Christmas presents). Remember: be brave, be yourself, and let other women be themselves, too. That's the important bit. Even the darkest nights brighten when the stars hold each other's hands.

Lots of love from your Aunty Amy xxx

THE little girl WHO GAVE ZERO FUCKS

Some days, the world was
meant to change.
Your thoughts go bang, your
eyes turn strange

Like a magnificently coloured
kaleidoscope lens,
No matter the hows and the whys
or the whens

As the mountains have peaks and the
seas have their waves,
Some days you just know you were
born to be brave.

Elodie-Rose was a girl on a mission
In a town where girls act like obedient
    kittens,

Sing soft the same tune and dance neat
    the same jigs,
Wear the same flowery dresses
    and pretty blonde wigs.

But Elodie-Rose vowed to change
    this old world
Because Elodie-Rose isn't like
    other girls.

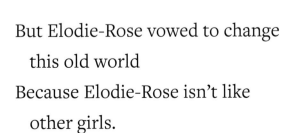

In this town, each morning's the same as before.

Girls wake up and wash, take their socks from the floor,

Eat breakfast, brush teeth, make the messy old bed,

Pack their lunchbox with snacks for the long day ahead,

Jump quick through the Lego, the dolls and toy trucks,

Open the wardrobe, grab their basket of fucks.

Wait: 'What are fucks?' you might suddenly cry

As you halt to attention and rub your wide eyes!

Well, fucks are the things that girls keep in their basket

And must give away when somebody asks it.

Fucks are their blues, their esteems and their happies,

Sat in their basket ever since they wore nappies.

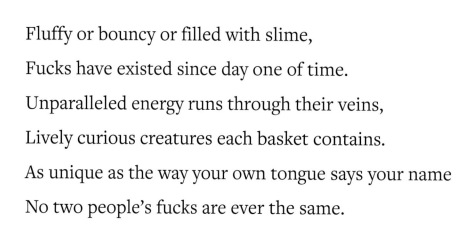

Fluffy or bouncy or filled with slime,

Fucks have existed since day one of time.

Unparalleled energy runs through their veins,

Lively curious creatures each basket contains.

As unique as the way your own tongue says your name

No two people's fucks are ever the same.

All girls bear the burden of fucks every day.

For when someone is mean or throws nasty their way,

If strangers start trouble or cause an upset

Their palm is outreached and a fuck they will get.

In the morning girls' baskets are full and stand tall,

But by bedtime there's no fucking fucks left at all.

When the sun sets, girls sleep, have the
  brightest of dreams

Of giraffes and quad biking and jelly and cream.

Becoming an astronaut or rich CEO –

To unlimited magical places they go.

Such sweet thoughts replenish their baskets of fucks,

So they rise once again, feeling up on their luck.

Yet with a new day, forever can start

With fire in your belly, such hope in your heart.

So Elodie-Rose made a plan not to care:

Those fucks in her basket were going nowhere!

Friends might call her crazy, a terrorist too,

But Elodie-Rose

Had wondered

And pondered

And thought it important

That when you have fucks,
Those fucks should
belong to just you.

Courageous, a soldier, such difference she yearned

To make to the words and the habits she'd learned.

But her mum had told her to play by the rules,

In houses and shops and in gardens and schools.

So, like clouds float in silence to make the rain fall,

Our girl left the house saying nothing at all.

Skipping to school, her young brain gave a buzz,

Arms tingling and shaking, breath short, just because

Thoughts diving and swimming within her today:

Is this normal? Does everyone else feel this way?

Like tornadoes move earth,

  make the air thick with dust,

She was puzzled, whilst walking

  to board the school bus.

But excitement was bubbling: she'd tell all her friends
Of the plans for the fucks and the baskets to end!
Waving madly, assuming these two girls had seen her –
One pal was named Marge and the other Edwina –
But rarely it happens, as you'll understand,
That reactions from others will go just as planned.

This morning their four eyes were black as black soot
Or like two mouldy grapes in a basket of fruit.
Pair of icy blue faces, contorted and stretched,
Greeted Elodie-Rose as she climbed the bus steps.
Said Edwina: 'I think you're wrong in the head.
I heard someone tell someone that someone had said.'

Marge nodded and tutted and furrowed her brow,
'We were best friends on Monday; we're not best friends now!'
'Don't ask any reasons,' they chorused and leered,
'Just that he said that she said that he said you're weird!'
Normally Elodie-Rose's pure dear heart would sink,
So preoccupied, girls, with what other girls think.

'Now move down the bus. There's no seats – you should stand!'
Marge grimaced and giggled and held out her hand,
Demanding a fuck from poor Elodie-Rose,
Who had pouted her lips and sat silent and froze.

Flighty bile of the bullies, she thought it unfair
And most often got mocked for her big frizzy hair.

In heatwaves most fucks were gone by double science,
Today, Elodie-Rose's curls slapped her face in defiance
As she shook her head back to the back of the bus
And peeped out of the window without any fuss.
Daydreamed about wizards and roses and stars,
Ignoring the bullies, Edwina and Marge.

Once again, this buzzing emerged in her mind.
Not thoughts for the girls who had been so unkind
But sensations inside, like her brain might combust.
Do all girls feel this way? Surely everyone must?
Best not mention, concluded Elodie-Rose.
Continued her journey . . . for now, the case closed.

* * *

Arrived at the school gates,
   a crowd of girls talking,
Focused on their feet and
   idly walking.
'My toes are too fat,' she
   heard one pupil say.
'I've eaten nothing this
   week, but they won't go
   away!'
'The magazines say tiny
   toes are in.'
'I flex them all day, but it
   won't make them thin!'

What peculiar statements, thought Elodie-Rose,
Who gazed at these girls and then at her own toes.
Were they fat? Were they thin? Clinically obese?
Were they filled with pure lard just like overfed geese?
Fingers reached for a fuck at the heft of her hooves,
Unwillingly dampened by insecure youths . . .

. . . But clowns have big toes and
  they all have a ball,
And rhinoceroses care little for toe size
  at all.
All these beauties with big paws completely
  content,
'If I hate both my feet then my fucks
  will be spent!

'As long as they'll
get me from
A to B,
My basket stays
full of my fucks
and my heart
remains free.'

Elodie-Rose marched along to her locker,

Heart beating and smashing like nothing could rock her.

Soon a boy in her class swaggered over real close,

Slyly tried to link arms with our Elodie-Rose.

Little girls should be good and enjoy boys' affections

Who don't like it when given a taste of rejection.

But Elodie-Rose
    didn't want this today.
She huffed and she puffed
    and she pushed him away.
'Please let my arm go,'
    she politely requested.
He took a step back,
    as she had suggested,

But instead of goodbye turned a
    bright shade of red!
He sneered and he snorted and
    flicked her forehead.

'DON'T FANCY YOU ANYWAY, YOU'VE EYES LIKE A TOAD!
YOUR HEAD'S FULL OF DANDRUFF, IT LOOKS LIKE IT SNOWED!
I WAS TOLD THAT YOU'LL HOLD ALMOST ANYONE'S HAND.
YOU'RE THE UGLIEST GIRL IN THE WHOLE OF THE LAND!'
As a lawyer in court lays down common sense,
Elodie-Rose went to make her defence.

Have you ever tried talking
 through heartache and sobs?
Wet tears splashing downward
 like big bluey blobs?

The weight of the world is the heaviest load –
Nobody wants toad eyes, not even a toad!
While the feels gripped her throat and stifled her
 voice,

Elodie-Rose realised
she had a choice.

Her ears could suck up all the bad words and noise,
Or ignore the lame things spat by insecure boys.
Those fucks stayed in her basket, a wonderful thing!
Feeling taller than ever, she started to sing:
'If a boy is mean or acts too keen
Or jealousy makes him turn bright
green!
It is very important not to give him
one of your fucks.
Because fucks are the most
important thing a little girl's got.'

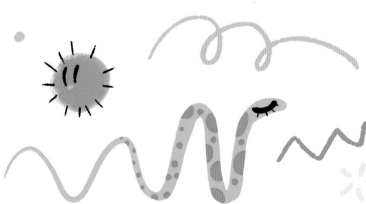

The buzzing once more stopped her right in her tracks
Like a hive of bees bumping their bottoms and backs.
Flying, whizzing inside from small ear to small ear,
How unusual, she mused, *when will this disappear?*
She told not a soul 'bout the buzzing that day,
For she hoped for the feeling to fly far away.

Funny how everyday
landscapes can alter
When your heart feels as
strong as the Rock of
Gibraltar!

An abundance of judgements
in one afternoon,
Now she noticed them all,
like a yellow balloon!

All these regular things
that she did as routine,
Opportunities now, to
stand up and be seen.

The dinner lady tutted at eating two cakes.
Art teacher fussed about mess she might make.

In assembly, head scolded and said to be silent.
In debating class, told off for being too violent.

In PE the team yelled at her to run faster.
In home economics, her soufflé a disaster.

Despite breaking rank and getting detention,
Keeping fucks in her basket remained her intention.

And while giving fucks is the world's persistence,
Not giving them made not a blind bit of a difference.

Elodie-Rose still had her brain and her laugh,
Her passport, her wonder, her whimsy, her daft!

But the oddest thing happened, a cherry on top . . .

When she gave zero fucks, adults' eyes would go pop!
Steam emerged from their ears like the front of a train,
Their faces would frazzle and mouths went insane.

Going utterly quackers
like a lake full of
ducks,
Because everyone
stares, and cares and
despairs at the little
girl who gives
zero fucks.

On release from school, much later
that day
She was energised, hopeful and
ready to play.
All at once felt disheartened, her
head became dizzy,
Girls flippantly throwing their
fucks like a Frisbee.

How she wished all these females would
get along sweetly,
Yet the scene on the playground
depressed her completely.

A million mouths shouting the nastiest names,
Friends feeling frustrated, misplacing the blame.

Accusing each other of too much make-up,
Gossiping freely on each other's break-ups.
Using words like 'fat' and 'spotty' and 'shrill'
Boring into their pride like a pneumatic drill.

Pinches and punches and
pulling of hair,
Swinging their arms like
a ride at the fair.

A million small girls all standing in tears,

Crushing their hopes and expanding their fears.

When you're stuck in the swamp all you see is
the muck

Where they'd taught one another to give all
their fucks.

Elodie-Rose ran home, through the leaves and
   the lanes,
Saw a little girl sat on the road: Sophie-Jane.
Her basket was empty, face littered with sad,
Looked up at Elodie-Rose as if she was mad!

'You're the girl with the full basket, you're crazy itself!
You shouldn't cause trouble, it's bad for your health.'

Elodie-Rose gave a shrug. 'I'm just being me.
It's been a strange day, but I'm fine, as you see.

'I've broken the rules but I'm not sent to prison,
My eyes are the brightest with sparkling vision!'
They both looked around: no policemen were hid,
None spying in bushes or crouched under bin lids.

Asked Sophie-Jane: 'So I can keep my fucks all day long?
I can stick to my guns and nothing goes wrong?

'Each night I must dream about wonderful things –

'Of the cheetah that sprints and
the bluebird that sings.

'The next morning I'm empty, my brain is alone
All my good dreams have left me, my memory's gone.'

'Well, it hasn't been easy,' Elodie-Rose admitted.
'It's been quite a test to stay strong and committed.
I've been bullied and grabbed and told off by teachers,
Told to be silent, laughed at for my features.
Doubt in my head and my brain won't stop whirring,
Butterflies in my tummy, like something is stirring.'

Squealed Sophie-Jane: 'I get that fizzing, too!
If I'm stepping outside of my normal, like you.
I think that it means that our brains are the best.
Let the buzzing remain and we'll teach all the rest!
Don't doubt yourself, sunshine, let's act as a team.
We'll help each other remember our dreams.'

'I'm no guru,' she mused to Elodie-Rose,
'But perhaps from personality, confidence
    grows?
        When I am myself, I have fun and
        I thrive.
        In fact, I'm the happiest girl alive!
        I won't tell anybody what to do
        But I wonder
        And ponder
        Now think it important
        That when you have fucks
        The one with those fucks should
        be you!'

My dears, some people were born to be bad.
They'll fight to extinguish the fire you had.
In a bucket of crabs, when one tries to climb out,
The rest pull his legs back with no shred of doubt.
Their collective ambition: remain in a cave,
Because crabs don't fancy their friends
   being brave.

It's nonsense and silly to worry of others –
We know not their history, their illness,
  their suffers.
The more you make stress on how twisted
  they are,
Your soul becomes smelly and gooey like
  tar.
Be strong, be kind, fix a smile on your face.
Give zero fucks and the world's a more
  positive place.

Sophie-Jane said sorry for calling her nuts,
Elodie-Rose gave forgiveness, no ifs and no
  buts.
 'Let's have lunch tomorrow, sit under the
  trees,
We'll eat chocolate cupcakes topped with
  melted cheese!'
Sophie-Jane swooned at the thought
  of their feast,
United, their friendship,
  in eating like beasts.

* * *

All at once, the buzzing began to stop;
The sound of the whirring started to
   drop.
They hugged and high-fived and
   whooped to the trees,
Forgetting the frenzy of internal bees.
Like birds stop and smile when to south
   they have flown,
Nobody needs to be brave on their own.

Elodie-Rose's mum was at the front door,
She'd heard of the soufflé, debating and more.
The headmaster phoned, up in arms at the rebel,
Her bad behaviour – he said – had been next level.
'My, my, Elodie-Rose! Your basket is filled!
It's the end of the day, yet nothing has spilled?'

Elodie-Rose instinctively hung her sweet head.
'Do you think I'm weird, Mum, must you send me to bed?'
With a purse of the lips and a screw of the nose,
Mum moved close to inspect Elodie-Rose.
Her daughter was worried her eyes would go pop!
That if love was an ocean, she'd drunk the last drop.

Instead, her mum cheered and clapped her hands,
So proud of her girl who'd taken a stand!
She hugged until she could hug no more,
Picked Elodie-Rose from her feet off the floor,
They whirled and twirled, couldn't keep it all in
Like two dancing squirrels who'd drunk too much gin!

'When I was young I gave my fucks to all,
To boys and teachers, short and tall,

'Taxi drivers, tarantulas, celebs
    and bosses
Who took my fucks and
    enjoyed my losses.
What I wouldn't give to go
    back in time,
Keep hold of my fucks so my
    fucks were all mine.

'If an enemy tells you how to feel
Or judges when you eat a meal,
They crave your thunder, swipe and steal:
Give zero fucks, like no big deal!
The sun shines to make us
    warm as toast,
So save fucks for those who
    need it most.

'Look to those who have no voice,
Born without riches and live without
    choice.
Think of those who need support,
Act as kindly as you've been taught.

'A pearl lies beneath
    the hardest shell,
So find your shine and
    use it well.'

WELL!

Elodie-Rose's basket was overflowing,
Her spirits high and aura glowing.
And all of a sudden, because she was able,
She reached for a candle from the dinner table.
Set her basket on fire so fucks filled the room!
They grew and they flew, they
blossomed and bloomed.

Fluffy fucks zoomed from the window's edge
Out into the garden, crashed through
  the hedge,
Knocked on the doors of every girl in town,
Removed from their basket so boring and brown.
And lo and behold the girls realised
That fucks could be saved right
  in front of their eyes!

How peculiar this, to be suddenly free,
To act how they act and be who they . . . BE!
Some days, the world was meant to change
Your thoughts go bang, your eyes turn strange
Normality bursts, you're never the same
And bravery saves your bustling brain.

And as sure as in winter the good wind blows
This hurricane day soon drew to a close.
The sun did set, the moon did peep
And Elodie-Rose knew it was time to sleep.
So what dreams that night would she discover
Tucked up tight under the duvet cover?

That night, as the pillow hugged our hero's head,
Hooting owls led her away from bed.
And although dreaming, she felt wide awake

As her little knees knocked and began to shake.
Wriggling and running through puffs of smoke,
That made her cough and splutter and choke.

A force took her floating through spooky mist,
Dark mysterious woods with turns and twists.
Trees started talking and flapping their sticks,
Bats appeared, such a nightmare, mind playing tricks!
Then Elodie-Rose heard a screaming, high-pitched,
Cackling traditional sounds of a witch.

Winds whispered out loud as she fretted and feared:
All at once through the fogs, a woman appeared.

No black cape to be seen, warts or crooked nose,
This young maiden, dressed in regular clothes.
Beige rags, messy hair, no shoes on her feet.
'Hello, Elodie-Rose, it's a pleasure to meet!

'You gave zero fucks, what a wonderful day!
I'll tell you a story about me, if I may.
Once upon a time, I was a young girl like you
With so many things I wanted to do.

'My friends and I, such lives ahead of us,
Became inspired by being rebellious.

'Yet four hundred years ago, if we're counting,
A movement dark and cruel was mounting.
Thousands of women were silenced and hunted,
Seized and caged, imprisoned, affronted.
Our crime? For being born as girls
With button noses and hair in curls.

'A gaggle of men, driven by desire
To see us surrounded by flames and fire,
Would twist our legs and pierce our skin,
Starve us until we were scarily thin,

'Throw us in lakes to see if we'd float,
With water filling our lungs and throats.

'Dear Elodie-Rose, this happened to me.
I was loud and different and longed to be free.
Had mischievous thoughts, refused to marry,
It made some men around me wary.
I was tried and tested, branded a witch
Burned on a heap and dumped in a ditch.'

And now Elodie-Rose could hardly speak,
Tiny tears tumbling down her cheeks.
Stood in a wood with a witch's ghost
This dream was the dream she'd
    remember the most!
Soon crowds of other women
    came into view,
Big-haired, small-haired,
    bald-headed, too.

Some had freckles and others had cats,
A few wore trousers and a couple had hats,
Hairy legs for some, for others long chins
(In the middle ages, seen as sins!)
The common thread running all along:
None of these women had done anything wrong.

They joined together to issue a warning:
'Remember us all, tomorrow morning,
And Elodie-Rose, please never forget
The challenges won't be over yet.
For peculiar things happen if you're
    not the norm –
You refuse the rules and uniform.

'They'll laugh at you, chase you and tell you to stop.
Resist and watch their eyes go POP!
Imagine a new world, rich and robust . . .
Where we're all allowed to be completely us.
Like twigs stoke the fire that flickers and rages,
Stick up and stand up for girls through the ages.'

Elodie-Rose flew to new fantastic dreams
Shooting through her mind like laser beams!
Pictured pyramids, snorkels and purple hair,
Pop music, train rides and honey bears.
Eating seven-foot strawberries and chocolate pies,
Shark-swimming and winning the Nobel Prize.

And as witches would want for her and you,
Resolve to make these dreams come true.
Though ridiculous as your ideas may sound
Big things start from one thought profound.
Like the volcano knows it's meant to rise,
Possibilities explode for a girl who tries.

Next morning she wrote her dreams as a list,
And decided to craft a book just like this!
Announced to her mum as they drank a smoothie,
'Maybe they'll turn this into a movie!'
So enthused about her life's new road
Elodie-Rose didn't care if she'd eyes like a toad.

Licking butter and jam from her breakfast knife,
She'd set her fucks free for the rest of her life.
She'd march for girls both big and small
To be themselves and knock down walls.
No one's best and no one's worst
She and Sophie-Jane just got there first.

When you're being brave
  and nerves attack
Don't let your basket hold you back.
Your brain might buzz and feel so
  strange
But we all have strength to make
  things change.
Like the spark you feel
  when lightning's struck,

Elodie-Rose
Had wondered
And pondered
And thought it important
That the world . . . needs more little girls . . .
  who give zero fucks.

Author's acknowledgements

I'd like to thank myself, very much, for persevering.

Anna. Your wonderfulness, support and honesty are unparalleled. Thank you for telling me to write a poetry book and for having such natural authority that I did it without question, purely to impress you. As a human being you'll always be my benchmark of brilliance. Well done, yeah?

To Mum and Dad. You must be so proud! Thanks for being an excellent pair, for loving me enough to let me be crazy and for acting shocked, yet supportive, every time I read my book to you. If I make any money from this, I'll take you both to Oxford again. If not, then this acknowledgement will have to do.

To Laura and Louise. I've been very lucky to have you both as role models. Thank you for showing me that anything and everything is possible if I just get off my big fat ass and do it. You've taught me ambition, resilience and you are probably to blame for my personality.

Bethan. Thank you for helping me with Instagram! Make sure you and your friends keep arguing with all the idiots because that's the only way stuff will change (and don't let the fuckers gaslight you – it's totally possible to be angry and happy at the same time).

Sophie. Thank you for letting me turn you into a character! You may not look quite like her, or be ready to read the words out loud, but you're the living embodiment of this book and that makes me very proud.

To Nicole. The Sophie-Jane to my Elodie-Rose! (Not just because she's a person of colour, that's just a happy coincidence.) *starts banging fist on the bus window* FRIDAY NIGHT AT THE CLUB AND IT'S FUCKING MENTAL! MOVE FROM THE PUB TO THE CLUB FOR SOME AWESOME SOUNDS!

Franny Franbo! I had to get drunk to write this message. What a wonderful friend you are: you helped me so much and never threw it back in my face for emotional blackmail purposes. I can't wait until I turn this book into a film and give you front row tickets to the first screening and then invite you up on stage for the Q&A afterwards.

To Hoshi for being the first person to EVER read this! I'm so happy you cried. It spurred (and turned) me on more than you can imagine.

John, you now officially own me which is what you've wanted ever since we were eighteen years old, you absolute sicko.

Stephen! Well. What an intro. I literally couldn't have done this without you and am forever grateful for all your support, always. Although I'd never say that anywhere other than here, right now.

Bea. So many LOLs about this on so many levels. But thank you for everything (and say sorry again to you-know-who!).

Dtown and Jack. A million appreciations for the pep talks aplenty when I went a little mad during the crowdfunding process. I blame lack of sleep and also my general attitude to things.

To Jem. Thank you for reading the thing that I wrote and turning it into a work of art. You're a rare, inspirational talent and have created something perfect. I'm in awe!

Rishi, Cazbo, Ginge, Sim, Kelly, Gemma, Sam, Jemima Daisy . . . Thank you for your eyes and brains and nice words while I was trying to get this shit published. AND SIM YOU'LL GET YOUR FUCKIN' TOTE BAG SOON OK, CHILL OUT. Friends are great, I love mine. Thank you so much to all the amazing friends I don't have space to mention but who bought and shared the book: special thanks to Miranda, Ian, Mark, Eva, Cat, Hemant and Giles who went over and above. I'll be forever grateful for your pledgetastic contributions.

And most of all, I'd like to thank Beyoncé. Of all the centuries in the history of time, I was lucky enough to co-exist on your planet, and that's really cool.

Illustrator's acknowledgements

For Ben, Kit, Pooka and Julia, who always encourage me to give zero fucks.

Unbound is the world's first crowdfunding publisher, established in 2011.

We believe that wonderful things can happen when you clear a path for people who share a passion. That's why we've built a platform that brings together readers and authors to crowdfund books they believe in – and give fresh ideas that don't fit the traditional mould the chance they deserve.

This book is in your hands because readers made it possible. Everyone who pledged their support is listed below. Join them by visiting unbound.com and supporting a book today.

Kasper Aaquist Johansen	Pedro Avery	Pili Barrio	Jessie Blackledge
Phil Adams	Awkward Pisswhiskers	Chantelle Basford	Jo Blake
Adeline	James Aylett	Suzy Bashford	Wayne Blodwell
Michael Agnew	Emma Bahl	Ashley Bateman	Sophie Boner
Mediah Ahmed	Regan Baillie	Wayne Baxter	Leila Borris
Mie Akune	Rosie Baird	Kirsty Beagley	Estie Boshoff
Leila Ali	Rosie Baker	Xanthe Bearman	Beatrice Boue
A Allan	Louise Baldwin	Suzanne Bearne	Carolyne Bourhis
Gwen Alwood	Ted Baldwin	Emma Bell	Kate Bradley
Christopher Anderson	Matt Ballantine	Bobbie Belle	Clare Bradshaw
Vanessa Andrews	Davina Balvack	Danielle Bennett	Richard W H Bray
Jane Angell	Gemma Bardsley	Katy Bennett-Richards	Denise Breslin
Ariadne & Aaron	Chris Baréz-Brown	Marco Bertozzi	James Brimsted
Kylie Arthur	Rachel Barnes	Neal Bhatnagar	Sarah Briones
Adrian Ashton	Elise Barnett-Carden	Patricia Bierley	Sarah Brooke
Regina Atienza	Nathalie Barnett-Carden	Charlotte Blackburn	Carlie Bryan

Ericka Bryant
Monica Buchan-Ng
Katherine Burr
Amber Burton
Joel Bushart
Noel Bussey
Craig Butler
Charles Cadbury
James Caig
Serena Calderisi
James Campbell
Alison Canlin
Xander Cansell
Caroline
Ann Carrier
Ali Carrington
Tara Carroll
Anne Carty
Tom Casswell
Hanna Chamberlain
Adam Chappa-Chap
Hemant Chauhan
Julia Cheot
Brydon Cheyney
Ms Lily Chrywenstrom
Stephanie Claxton
Nic Close
Garrett Coakley
Hollie Cobb
Will Cooper

Victoria Coppin
Elizabeth Corbin
Katie Coteman
James Coulson
Ana Luiza Couto
Gemma Cowin
Kate Cox
Elodie Cronin
Deborah Crook
Karen Cross
Crowd Emotion
Lucy Croxford
Julia Croyden
Angela Crump
Gill Cummings
Alison Cutler
Irene D.
Jim Darby
Rishi Dastidar
Jess Davey
Lily Elizabeth Davies
Becca Day-Preston
Paul Dazeley
Alexei de Berner
Marie de Ortega
Emma Deacon
Richard Dean
Maren Deathlovezen
Sofia Dellera
Trish Denham

Matthew Desmier
Caro Devotchkita
Roopa Dhawan
Paul Dibble
Laura Dickinson
Miranda Dimopoulos
Qubra Din
Roz Dineen
Rachel Doherty
Jim Dowling
Simone Drinkwater
Sophie Drummond
Everly Jane Dudley
Ruth Duffy
RJ Duggan
Gemma Dunn
Lizzie Eckardt
Claire Eden
Danny Edwards
Giles Edwards
Rob Edwards
Sebastiaan Eldritch-Böersen
Michael Elliott
Nick Ellis
Henry Elliss
Bridgeen England-Wood
Jessica Enright
Michelle Erwin
Eric Eslinger
Kate Evans

Victoria Evans
Katie Evetts
Julie Fairman
Joan Fakra
Louise Farrow
Pete Fellows
Ashley Ferguson
Lara Ferreira
Sally Fincher
Hanna Fisher
Sadie Fitch Kempner
Kat Fletcher
Cliff Fluet
Jacob Flygenring
Frances Foley
Shri Footring
Anna Foster
Clare Fowler
Sarah Francis
David Freeman
Robert Freer
Imke Frylinck
Sara Full
Carli Furman
Greg Fyans
Susan Gadsby
Ken Gaffney
Beatrice Galilee
Raquel Galindo
Beth Gammon

Emily Gane
Nicole Garnier
Paula Geraghty
Wendy Gibbons
Jo Gibson
Rebekah Gierlinska
Nina Gill
Rhoanna Glenn
Lauren Goddard
Carli Gooch
David Goodall
Isabelle Goody
Lola Gosling
Caitlin Graham
David Graham
Shannon Graham
Arjan Gravemaker
Gillian Greeanaway
Mel Gregory
Dee Grice
Eva Grimmett
Jonny Fuckin' Grubin
Anne-Sophie Guerin
Sarah Guest
Hamid Habib
Claire Hagen
Kayt Hall
William Hamer Jones
Deborah Hance
Steven Hance

Rachel Hands-Portman
Kathryn Hardaway
Nora Hardwick
Sarah Hargreaves
Lyndsey Harris
Wayne Harris
Amélie Haudiquet
Emma Hazell
Toby Hemming
Dorte Henriksen
Fleur Hicks
Alex Hill
Natalie Hillier
Zarina Holmes
Emma Hopton
Sandy Hubert
Claire Hugman
Tess Hulme
Marivic Idanan
Mirona Iliescu
Patricia Irvine
Lara Izlan
Candice Jenkins
Katie John
Sophie Johnson
Cadi Jones
Rachna Julka
Be Kaler
Yush Kalia
Amy Kean

Eileen Kean
Laura Kean
Louise Kean-Wood
Kevin Keane
Mary Keane-Dawson
Jon Kershaw
Kiron Kesav
Dan Kieran
Will King
Fiona Kirlew
Jamie Klingler
Amanda Koster
Jai Kotecha
Alex Kozloff
Aparna Krishnan
Klara Krok-Paszkowska
Jessica Kuhlmey
Preeti Kumar
Ketan Lad
Lamara
Sally Lane
Suzi Laoudikos
Max Latimer
Laura
Leah & Leon
Amy Leather
Jack Leather
Emilia Lehvonen
Jay Leonard
Stephen Lepitak

Tim LeRoy
Mel Leslie
Dot Lethbridge
Ben Liebman
Justine Ming-Ching Lim
Estee Lingard
Penelope Lipsham
Michael Litman
Elizabeth Little
Robert Loch
Kerry Lock
Angeline Lodhia
Gillian Logie
Katherine Long
Josh Luckhurst
Ailsa Mackenzie
Chiara Maddocks
Sara Joy Madsen
Gautham Maediratta
Saba Mahmood
Jakeena Malli
April Mallory
Justine Bridget Malone
Kevin Malone
Hedy Manders
Amy Manning
Milcah Marcelo
Jemima Marchant-Smith
Kay Martin
Sarah Martin

Martyn

Abbie Mason

Amy Mason

Amy Matthews

Kieron Matthews

Ian McClellan

Scott McCombs

Andy McCormick

Anton McCoy

Leanne McCrory

Gracious McDuff

Charlotte McEleny

Aidan McQuade

Bairbre Meade

Stephen Meister

Sarah Melhuish

Nick Mellish

Sara Meltzer

Presley Alan Merchant

Daisy Meredith

Jo Merrett

Jonathan Mew

Carol Middleton

Howard Milton

Jay Milton

Rosie Milton

John Mitchinson

Laurie Modell

Rik Moore

Mark Mordey

Robin Morley

Sara Moulton

J. L. Munn

Byron Munson

Cate Murden

Logan Murray

Carlo Navato

Charlotte Neville-Rolfe

Leann New

Emily Newell

Jai Newton

Ann Ann Ng

Jocelyn Nguyen

Al Nicholson

Gary Nicol

Tom Nield

Carolyn Nisbet

Sam Norgate

Louisa North

Stephen North

Richard Noton

Lou Nylander

Francesca O'Connor

Moses O'Hara

Marie O'Meara

Edel O'Regan

Lili O'Donnell

Andy Oakes

Richard Oakley

Sam Oakley

Amy Oliver

Tom Ollerton

Nadiya Omar

Emma Osborne

Anna Pagan

Isabel Paredes

Hoshi Parr

Phillippa Payne

Loretta Pearce

Karen Pembroke

Debbie Penfold

Quentin Perrot

Helen Perry

Dan Peters

Siobhan Peters

Sarah Wooler Pickles

David Pidancet

Hannah Platts

Ian Plenderleith

Natasha Plowman

Joyce Po

Justin Pollard

Beki Pope

Lizzie Poppy

Mike Potts

Joanna Poulton

Joanne Price

Gary Pyke

Harriet Pyper

Edward Qualtrough

Marleen Raaijmakers

Emma Radcliffe

Anjali Ramachandran

Anna Randles

Clare Reddington

Alice Rees

Louise Reid

Geraldine Reilly

Mike Reynolds

Debra Rhodes

Paul Richards

Miriam Rieck

Christian Rieger

Jo Rigby

Ralph Risk

Sarah Rivett

Joey Rixson

Zara Roberts

Michelle Robinson

Rachael Robinson

Vikki Ross

Catherine Rossi

Alice Roughton

Charlotte Rowland Vanderzee

Kelly Rush

Rachel Sadler

Zoe Sadler

Clara Saladich

Ian Samuel

Claire Sanger

Robin Schonemann
Anya Searle
Melinda Seckington
Becky Selbie
Julie Selby
Eliza Sells
Persa Shadnia
Shan
Clare Sharp
Jasmine Sharp
Lucy Sharp
Saffron Sharp
Karen Sheard
Christine Siddall
Rebecca Siler
Emma Simmons
Caroline Simpson
Frankie Singler
Gena Sluga
Emma Smith
Julia Smith
Kerrie Smith
Nicola Smith
Susan Sneddon
Erik Sol
Scott Sprinkles
John Sreetharan, Mymedia
Amanda Steimberg

Maya Stephani
Gavin Stirrat
Emma Jane Stone
Katie Stowell
Nick Stringer
Sueguiney
Lucy Sullivan
Susie
Olga Sych
Alicja Syska
Melissa Tang
Joanna Tapio
Helen Tarver
Bobby Tay
Deb Taylor
Jeremy Tester
Rajvir Thakore
Claire Thomas
Ruby Thomas
Dorothy Thornton
Luke Tilly
Mark Tipper
Cliff Toghill
Claire Toland
A., E., & P. Toups Dugas
Kate Tresnan
Zosia Hannah Trup
Cat Turner

Sandra Turner
Sarah Turnham
Donna Valenzano
Marije van Akkerveeken
Michelle Van Ellis
Sasha van Spall
Gustavo Vas Falcao
James Vespa
Marisa Victoria
Victoria
Georgina Vizor
Hedwig Vollers
Jo W
Verity Waington
Alina Waite
Ashlea Walker
Jack Wallington
Rachael Wass
Imogen Watts
Oded Watts
Andy Way
Meghan Weatherill
Jo Webster
Isla Summer Weeden
Tina Wellers
Andrew West
Ava West
Rebecca West

Helen Westcar
Caroline Westgate
James Whatley
Nik Wheatley
Jane Wheeler
Douglas Whelpdale
Natalie Whitehead-Farr
Helen Wilding
Cat Williams-Treloar
Zoë-Elise Williamson
Rachel Ellen Wilmshurst
Anna Wilson
Keeley Wilson
Simran Wirk
Caryn Wolfe
Sarah Wood
Heather Woodbridge
Zoe Woods
Steve Woodward
Barney Worfolk-Smith
Melanie Woytiuk McKay
Jon Wright
Annette Yates
J L Yates
Silke Zetzsche